In the Abyss of My Wounds

Vaidehi Lachheta

BookLeaf Publishing

India | USA | UK

To my exceptional parents -

I give you your daughter.

The eye, alone in its socket, doesn't even know there's another one, just like it, an inch away, just as hungry, as empty.

— Ocean Vuong

Preface

You are about to dive into a world that is entirely mine—a mosaic of emotions, memories, and thoughts woven together across these pages. Each piece is drawn from the deepest corners of my being and comes from a different walk of life, reflecting moments of love, loss, hope, and despair. As you journey through this collection, it is my hope that you find fragments of yourself within it as well.

stains of the unsaid

If I were to be shot right now,
I'd hope my brains on this *sangemarmar* wall
would scream the enormity of my love—
a love so vast, it bred disgustingly selfish
desires
that took root in its soil.
I'd hope the humiliation of this skin
runs like water down the marble,
telling everyone it was heavy yet fleeting—
a veil that could never define me,
though it fought wars trying to.
I'd want it to show the flowers I kept alive,
the tenderness I held close,
even with blood-stained hands.
It couldn't consume me,
not fully—not ever.

Let the flies that once hummed in the corners
of my mind—
those restless thoughts of escape—
finally find light and air.
But I pray my loved ones never see them rise,
never know how often I wanted to flee
from everything that came too close.
If my brains were to paint this *sangemarmar*
wall,
I'd hope the world could trace the
dismembered membranes,
forming a map of all I cherished,
all I yearned for,
and all the apologies I carried but never gave
voice to.
Let the threads that bind this lifeless tissue
bear fruit—fat, purple figs of lives I couldn't
live.
Not the fragile ego I wore as a mask.
And as the figs dangle, heavy with meaning,
I'd hope the world plucks them gently,
one by one,
giving form to the intangible dreams I left
behind—
before they fall, bruised and forgotten,

to the ground.

dreams of paths beyond the street

At 9:00, the air was thick with heat and noise.
The city stretched awake, yawns hidden in honking horns.
Lorries rumbled forward, indifferent.
I stood still, caught in the endless cycle of waiting—
For the amber light to turn green.
The sun, relentless, bronzed faces and dreams alike.
And there he was, barefoot on melting asphalt,
A boy no older than six,
Holding a brown bag in one hand,
The other balancing a bundle of yesterday's news.
He darted between cars, weaving through impatience,

His small frame lost among polished glass and
metal.
Eyes searching, not for safety, but for
opportunity—
A pair of rupees, a nod of acknowledgment,
Perhaps a glance that didn't look through
him.
His shirt, threadbare, clung to his back.
The day's sweat mixing with layers of dust.
Was he looking for a brother in the chaos?
Or carrying the weight of a mother's absence?
He pressed a newspaper to a window,
"Today's headlines," his voice cracked but
steady.
A man in a pressed suit waved him away.
The boy flinched, stepping back—
Then turned, finding another window to try.
In the distance, an engine roared,
A signal blared, shooing him off the road.
He ran, clutching coins as if they were
miracles,
Then stopped—his face breaking into joy.
His brother stood at the edge of the crowd.
They embraced, bodies too small for their
burdens.

The traffic surged forward, and I drove away,
A reluctant cog in the machine of progress.
That night, I thought of his hands,
Small, creased, and too familiar with work.
Hands meant for clay and crayons,
Now carrying yesterday's stories to strangers.
What stories did his smile conceal?
What dreams did his hunger betray?
I learned something in that moment of
stillness:
Not everything can wait for better times.
This life—brief and burning—
Demands more than just survival.
It calls for notice, for care, for change.
And I regret, most of all,
That I didn't stop to ask his name.

please save me from
myself, ma

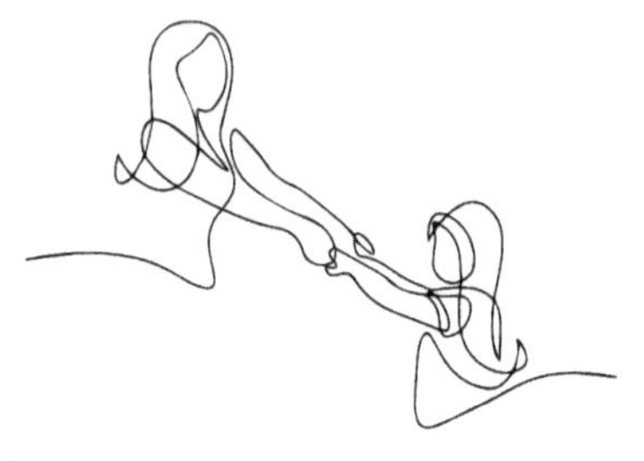

You made me, Ma.
Like a monarch butterfly,
I kept returning—
no matter how many dead bodies
of my kin I crawled over.
Each winter, I hoped for a new season,
for rebirth.

They say the universe makes you
live through something,
again and again,
until you learn to do otherwise.
Is it the earth's rebirth, then?

The journey back home
made me cleverer each time—

a rebirth of me,
a redefinition of me.

I am not a monarch.
I am human,
my blood a mix of freedom and community,
family lost somewhere in between.
You, however,
I carry with me,
like my pain—
unlike the way your mother carried me.

What do you see when you look at me, Ma?
That question scratches my mind more
with each passing winter.
Unfulfilled dreams,
a daughter not as beautiful as you,
just a burden.

For a while,
I thought I was missing something—
maybe our bond lived between the lines.

But my blood remains thirsty—

partly because your eyes are empty between
those lines,
partly because no one else is coming.

So, even in my distance,
I long.

My blood is finite.
I will long until it exhausts.

The tragedy, then,
is in my heart.
I wish you could see right through me, Ma,
the way you say you do.

current grocery list

I wake up,
Granola for fiber,
Yoghurt for protein,
Berries for antioxidants—
I tell myself, never skip breakfast.

By 2 p.m.,
I consume health by the bowl.

But I consume guilt by the bowl,
Consume anti-culture by the bowl,
Consume my mother's words
By
The
Bowl—
Like clockwork

Of a faulty clock.

I digest remarks,
Add more greens to my cart,
Eat my weight,
Cry my weight,
Hate my weight.

"Gym tomorrow," I say,
compare.

If only this stomach were gone—
Compare,
Compare.

I need more discipline,
Compare,
Compare,
Compare.

Sleep too much,
Still not enough.
Wake up at 1:59 p.m.,
The only thing I hear—
Never skip breakfast.

my anger is a gift from my father

My anger is 13 years old, Papa—
It weighs heavier
Than the first time I made you cry.

I am holding on to too much.
Can I put it down?
Moisture from flowers,
Color from paintings,
Daughter from mother,
In the broken glass vase of you.

No, please—
Time is of essence.
Essence remains
Of me.

I wonder what it is—
Lessons repeat.

My anger's first words were "Run away."
She knew what she wanted,
Restless.

I wish a hug were tighter,
Those eyes softer,
Words audible.

My anger grows hungrier—
It wants to save my mother
And to mother my father.

You can be soft.
You don't have to carry the weight
Of the world on your shoulders.

My anger is a sinner—
I wear it like a badge of independence.
I think, therefore I am, I think.

I try to leave it,
With a chain around my ankle,

A glass of wine and a cigarette in my hand.

My anger makes love with Lady Midnight—
Whimpering, anchorless,
Mourning the loved, the lost,
The loved and lost.

I yearn, therefore I am.
I love, therefore I am.
I enrage, therefore I am.

My anger begs to be extinguished—
A daughter's curse fuels it.
I destroy myself.

I am worthy.
I don't have a knife to my neck.
I am.

My anger was a gift from you, Papa.
I grow tired of your disappointed eyes—
Dissociate to love fully.

I need to put my anger to rest.
I am not a work in progress—

I am a vessel made of stone.

My anger is my friend.
I forgive you.

do you feel it too?

You must think the smile I wear hides pain—
Pain of shifting seasons,
Life cloaked in time, cloaked in seasons.
The pain of fading sunlight on sunflowers
each spring,
A season again, a cycle.
Pain of people leaving—
Their thoughts, their flesh, their tears drifting
away.
Pain of this fractured world—
The girl next cage, the boy who couldn't rage
Against the illogical neverland of perfect.
And I must say—you thought right.
It is pain, yes,

Or perhaps contentment, masked as pain.
But this pain?
It isn't born from the decay of societal
dignity,
From institutions that etch themselves into
me.
No, this pain belongs to something else.
It lives in the whispers of talks and touches,
The kind I've hoarded in the verses of this
play.
Touches that exist beyond flesh,
Beyond words—
In eyes deep enough to hold galaxies,
With eyes deep enough to mirror them back.
It has to do with the collision of sex and
cosmos,
When emotion transforms into language.
And those words?
Oh, those words—so powerful they dissolve
Into the fading sunlight on sunflowers each
spring.
For this pain, like the seasons,
Can be felt by all,
Understood by a few,
And cured by none.

unwavering nights

Save the girl child, the banners declare,
But their cries ring hollow in the stifling air.
What about the ones who are lost in the dark,
Swallowed whole before they can even start?
She told her father she would make him
proud,
Her voice trembling with dreams too delicate
to hold.
But the city, with its unforgiving streets,
Took her hopes and left her cold.
Her path was shadowed by lurking threats,
Every corner holding eyes that stripped her
bare.
The wind, warm and heavy, carried no
comfort,

Only the sharp edge of her silent despair.
Her hazel eyes stayed low, her gaze fixed on
the dirt,
As memories of the nights before weighed her
down.
The rhythm of footsteps grew louder behind
her,
Hands reaching, tearing at the fragile walls
she built.
She screamed, but the darkness swallowed her
voice,
The trees stood silent, the night unmoved.
This was not the first time,
And she knew it would not be the last.
She stayed quiet—not out of fear,
But to protect her mother,
Who once called her a fighter,
But never imagined battles like these.
She would not shatter her family's name,
Not in a place where honor
Could mean the death of truth.
She refused the courts, the scriptures,
The cameras that would reduce her pain
To a headline, a fleeting spectacle.
She would not be their martyr,

Nor the nation's broken child.
She gathered the broken pieces of herself,
Grateful her trembling legs still held her
weight.
Her breath was proof she hadn't been taken
completely, yet—
Hoping one day to rise above the shadows,
But the road calls her still, dark and endless,
Its whispers cruel, its grasp unyielding.
She knows she will return,
Her tears mixing with blood,
Her soul cast aside like scattered dust.
For these are the roads no one dares to name,
Where banners flap against the wind in vain,
And the world turns its gaze elsewhere,
Leaving her to dissolve into silence.

whose story is the most painful of them all?

Not a word.
Not even a syllable
Of how it all unraveled
Has ever echoed in these valleys—
Valleys of stories.
For words lose meaning
When all you hold is a fragment,
When you twist truths to fit your hands,
When you feel yourself breaking.
You. Not the valleys.
These valleys will know only rocks
Until trees claim them next monsoon.
They will know only dirt
Until water bends, caresses their jagged edges,
And makes love to their scars.

They will know only thunder
Until the right cloud pours life into their
cracks.
Yet you wander into them, in this heat,
Seeking peace, seeking answers.
You forget the rain that stirs within you,
How you've longed to drown—
Not to vanish,
But to feel it fully,
To let it touch you
Without stealing your essence.
But you forget:
A little theft is part of the gift.
You were made to break,
To fracture just enough
To see the stardust within.
You forget the heat will fade.
You forget the dirt has always nurtured
answers.
You forget yourself—but not entirely.
Why not remember by losing this time?
Why not let the tongues speak their truths,
Just this once?
Why not let the stories flow—
Stories that will echo in these valleys,

Stories the earth will crave like rain,
Stories to awaken life in the waiting soil.

Vipassana

It's a tale of trees, not the seas
For the skies never seemed to take their
Eyes off of the greens that swayed beneath
them.
A tale of a lost evening—
Heavy air, crickets' hum,
Warm winds and minds adrift.
Our desires mirrored the sky
As the moon and our smiles grew clearer,
And the sun began its retreat
From green maidens to the queen sea,
Back with our restlessness,
Our collective fears,
Our choices,
Our pasts,
Our lives,

Lives...
If there were,
If they still remained,
Or if the promised rebirth happened in an
alternate dimension.

Perhaps the sun fell in love with the maidens,
Radiating everything they never asked for,
Everything they had to take—
Thrown at them,
Made to endure—
Because, like this world,
The sun misunderstood love.

Or was it strengthening us?
Because the dark was an illusion—
The storm before the promised light,
Really our own reflection,
Finally visible after all this time?
Something in silence that occupied us,
hallucinated us,

Until we heard the final, soothing gong—
And we were free.
Free to do everything,

Or so we thought.

Why, then, does the world look unchanged?
Why is the sun so cruel,
The moon so distant?
Why all this noise?

We tell them we love them,
But they receive it like the moon—
Constantly shifting,
Never still,
So close yet so far.

We tell them we respect them,
Like the sun respects the queen,
But the sun became cruel when it radiated
too much,
And the queen couldn't hold it, couldn't keep
it forever.

But, yes—
The rebirth did come,
Not of the body,
But of the soul.

things I carry with me

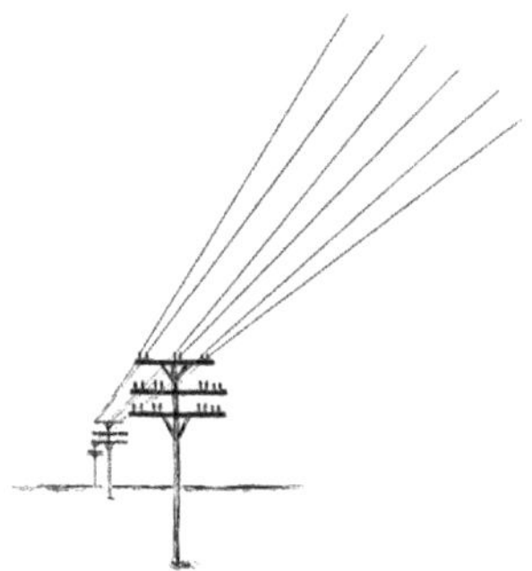

New year packing list -

1. A list of therapists near me—because any moment now, I might gather the courage to face what I fear most.
2. A brochure for a chiropractor—my body, mind, and soul are all out of alignment.
3. A lighter—not for me, but to trade for a puff of a stranger's cigarette and the meaning of their name in their native tongue.
4. Crayons—for blank walls that beg for color; being a "good kid" never took me anywhere.

5. Every letter ever written to me—proof that I've left a fleeting, better mark on someone else's life.
6. A Spotify link of songs that stirred something in me, and sunscreen—because the sun deserves to see me dance.
7. Keys to a house whose walls will one day outlive my secrets, erasing them like whispers in a few hundred years.
8. Pepper spray—to guard against the evil eye.
9. An antacid and an empty stomach—for the endless flavors the world offers.
10. A painkiller—so I can better disguise the truth that my soul never outgrew my twelve-year-old body, even if the rest of me did.
11. A lipstick—to soften the sting of words that would otherwise burn me from the inside out.
12. And a napkin—for when grief doesn't ask permission before it spills out in public places.

keertan

As I wander the terrace, the night unfolds,
My thoughts disrupted, the silence scolds.
A distant prayer begins its climb,
Its echo weaves through space and time.
The tablas, santoors, and gongs arise,
Their rhythms tempting, their beats precise.
A melody flows, both fierce and sweet,
As hearts align with its pounding beat.
They long to escape, to feel no more,
To lose themselves where sound will soar.
The crescent moon can wait its turn,
While their restless souls begin to burn.
Moved by the rhythm, their spirits depart,
Bound in the spell of this heavenly art.
I watch, and a thought takes root in me:
The closer you come, the less you see.
The more you seek the crowd's embrace,
The more of yourself you will erase.

guide my tension

From the safety of the tinted glass, I watch
you,
Unaware of how your gaze disrobes me—
A fruit ripened in your longing,
Its sweetness just out of reach, its skin a
secret.
Your lips move as if tasting me in thought,
A kiss veiled behind the shadow of your
lashes.
Your hands tighten, betraying the hunger you
suppress,
Veins straining against the weight of your
desire.
And I?

I grin, caught between disbelief and
fascination,
At how fiercely I've learned the language of
you—
And how fiercely you yearn to decipher me.

cue The Doll People by Sofia Isella

I have been touched in places
you would never dare to name,
while you have been caressed in the spaces
where I ache to be known.

In the darkness,
it seeps into me—
a hunger in the hollowed parts I never knew
existed,
in the corners I wish could vanish.

Life has sculpted me in cruel hands,
and these polished, well-dressed souls
have mocked the remnants of who I am—

bodies the same,
but hearts carved from different stone.

I move through days,
burying a past in the folds of my skin,
in a world where they pay
to taste the bitter sweetness of someone else's
emptiness,
searching for fleeting pleasure,
chasing moments that never stay.

And somewhere along the way,
I became that someone—
the shape they mold to fit their longing,
and I, too, am shaped,
losing pieces of myself
with each encounter.

mother earth

There is something strange about this rain—
It is not merely water condensing again.
It is Earth herself, I believe,
Trying to cry out through her grief.
She screams, her voice soaked in despair,
Her tears clinging to our clothes, our air.
Clouds collide, growling like beasts,
A raw, feral roar that drowns our peace.
But where, within your walls,
Will you hear her calls?
The whole settlement falls silent,
An empty room to echo her torment.
Like a child, she shouts, again and again,
Her voice a thunderclap that numbs your
veins.
You skip a beat, frozen in fear—
But you, unbothered, return to your gears.
This rain is no ordinary fall,

It bends your umbrellas, commands them to crawl.
Your vehicles cry, your rooftops plead,
Birds scatter as rivers swell and seethe.
The storm paints the land in blinding white,
Extinguishing your lights, gripping you in fright.
The moon watches with a distant glow,
Smiling at a daughter reclaiming what was hers, long ago.
I asked her then, as the tempest roared,
"Why this fury? What are you fighting for?"
She sighed, her voice soft yet wild,
"My child," she said, "I am your mother, defiled.
I do not wish to drown what I gave birth to—
But my screams are what you've forced me into.
These tears of mine, the floods you face,
Are the pain of a mother, misplaced."
I returned with an apology on behalf of all—
To the one who raised us, watched us fall.
But we turn deaf to her voice,
Straighten our raincoats, and march by choice.

And now, I believe, there's a pact,
A sacred bond the universe enacted:
"I govern you, give you breath and time,
I lend you a piece of my heart to climb.
But harm her, and I will tear you apart—
For though you wander, you do not own my heart.
I promised Earth, the day she grew life,
'When the waters rise and your pain takes flight,
When dirt consumes and you ache to heal,
Speak—and every ear will hear,
Every eye will weep, every soul will kneel.'"

on the experience of womanhood

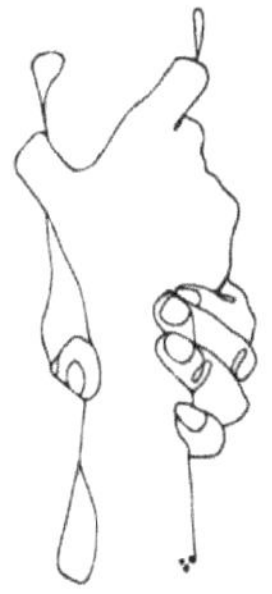

My neighbor and I wash dishes
at the same hour every day.
I know this because, as I rinse and stack,
lost in the rhythm of water and glass,
I glance to my left,
where she stands,
a reflection I've never met—
curly hair, glasses,
shoulders bowed under unseen weight.
I wonder what it would take
to see a man in her kitchen,
even once,
keeping her company,
if not her heart.

We've never met each other's gaze,
but I hope she feels me,
not as a shadow, but as a steady whisper:
I'm here.
The weight of the kitchen is no small thing.
Let the rhythm soothe you,
or let it slip away—
you aren't alone.
Do you dream of different times?
Of recipes shelved in your mind,
waiting for a day of solitude?
Do you crave sweetness?
I could bring you cake;
dessert is softer,
warmer,
when shared between women anyway.
You seem twice my age.
And while the love of my life
folds laundry beside me,
I wonder when the last man stood in your
kitchen,
not to take,
but to give.
My mother tells me her life
was spent in soapy water,
her dreams boiled away with the kettle.

I hope you don't feel the same.
But if you do—
look to your right.
You've got a friend.

migrate

And there goes another monsoon,
Sweeping away the heat, spreading love.
Somewhere, a mother cradles her child,
And slowly, the season drifts into stillness.
The world seems to hold its breath,
As days soften into gentle light,
While nights rest in quiet shadows.
The sky, however, rumbles and shakes,
And beneath it, a lone tree sways,
Sheltering a family, safe in their nest,
For now— resting before their journey west.
The world they leave behind ticks on,
As roses fade in the shrinking warmth.
And there they go, gliding beneath the
skyline,
Overexposed to the dimming light,
Carrying the weight of their quiet departure.

enlightenment

For me, the universe is like slices of bread,
Each piece feeding my pages that remain
unwritten.
I sprinkle glimmers of life on the shores of
weightlessness,
And within this ever-expanding unity,
I stand as a singular starkness.
I take the cosmic rays, twisting and turning
them,
Bending their invisibility into a radiant
storm.

I can count every atom of the earth and still
feel alone,
Yet, among the asteroids, I find a home.
I trace letters and words, even in the dark,

Turning fragments of the unseen into pure brightness.
I play with the flaming spheres of lightest elements,
And in all of this, I discover my own form of enlightenment.

when love shows up unannounced

A thought visits me often, heavy with unease:
What if you never come to love this skin of
mine—
The way it holds me together, yet fractures at
times?
What if the hairs I try to hide
Whisper their own stories when you least
expect them,
Or the absence of my second eyelid, tucked in
the folds,
Pushes you farther,
As my face becomes a map
Of all the places I've lived, uninvited.
What if the space between my brows

And the crooked path of my nose
Urge you to seek smoother roads?
What if the very lips you once kissed
Feel foreign,
The dimples not deep enough
To make you stay?
And when you move lower,
What if you find imperfections
Where once there was softness?
What if these marks of time,
Like ripples, pull you away,
Dimming the glow I once held?
But what if, despite all this,
I learn to claim this body—
The scars, the stretch,
The places the world failed to touch me,
Just as I am?
What if, in the end,
I become the kind of love
That has always eluded me?

fading echoes

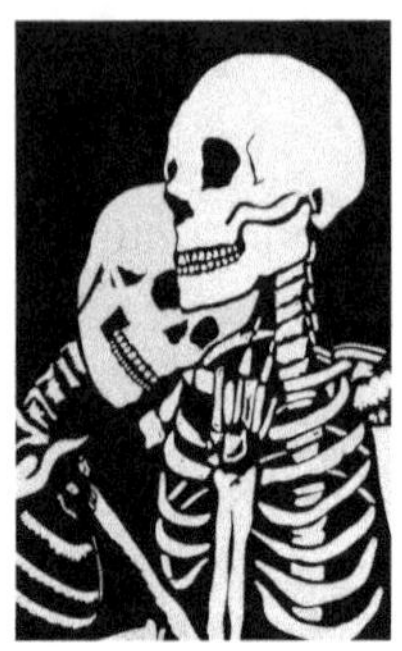

You are the shade to my scorching sun;
Toward you, I run and run.
But there is a melody, and the composer is
life,
And I can't hum it, even with all my might.
That chapter is over, and another page you
won't turn,
Until your next dream to life returns.

Standing empty in the dark,
Your glow is my only spark.
And I wished for that light,
For which I will fight and fight,
To know myself, to love both of us again.
But I find myself lost, far from that gain.

how to not live:

in the past

You go on,
Searching for paradise,
A horizon,
A *Sangam* of all that you've ever desired.
Trailing behind you is everything you've ever
touched,
And yet, you seem to swim toward the
desired,
As if it calls you.
It works, as though each wave was made
To carry you forward—
Except this one.
The wave of time.
It pushes the air from your lungs,

Forcing you to retrace every thought,
Or at least, it feels that way.
Every drop of it is a force in itself—
A blend of what you wanted and what you
feared,
A force of the senses and the soul.
Every other way of being seems to blur,
Or perhaps it only seems that way.
But weren't you always rising toward the
surface,
To gaze upon your desires?
Weren't you drowning in your own tears,
And yet still, somehow, you swam on?
Wasn't the sun setting to cast light on your
shadows?
Weren't your lungs filled with the salt of time,
Even before you knew it?
Weren't you crossing these waters for the very
purpose of it?
So, maybe it only *seems* that way.
For in order for this wave to relent,
You must learn to swim *with* it,
To move through it,
To become it—
And, in the end,

To defeat it.

the debt of love

I look at myself in the mirror when I cry,
as if the glass holds answers
my reflection might throw back at me.
I trace my body with weary eyes,
a familiar stranger,
stalling before I confront the ache within.
It's like seeing my thoughts
from a third person's view—
a third person who is still me,
but truer,
untouched by the distortions I feed myself.
The reflection just *is*.
Unfiltered, unyielding.
It knows no lies, no pretense.
It is me,

loud and bold,
its existence a silent love letter
I've been too afraid to read.
Perhaps that's why mirrors terrify me—
their honesty, their tenderness.
Perhaps that's why I linger too long,
as if caught between fear and hope,
finding reasons to love myself
that feel too vast to accept.
I almost grasp the answers
before I turn away,
because I haven't felt worthy of love in years.

I am limitless in november

I survived another November—
now what?
The ocean does not question its purpose.
Each wave moves as it must,
reaching the shore not with intent,
but inevitability.
Its meaning lies not in the arrival,
but in the weightless rhythm of being—
a motion untethered by expectation.
What would it take
to become like the ocean?
This November has settled into me,
heavier than the last,
the weight of passing time
etched deeper into my conscience.
I fear reaching my shore,

crushed under the burden of living,
my breath hollowed out
by unspent dreams.
But my shore deserves to see me whole,
to feel my feet dancing toward it.
I deserve to greet it
with love instead of regret,
to arrive not emptied,
but overflowing.
If the ocean could think,
would it mourn its endless cycles?
Or would it find freedom
in the absence of reason?
Perhaps that is the secret—
to exist as water,
as air,
as the quiet echo of all things past,
unshackled by purpose,
alive only in the flow.

23rd birthday cake

I have stopped myself through every hour I've
breathed,
Caged my spirit behind bars only I could see.
I kept my innocence at bay, wary of being
naive,
I took as little space as possible,
But none of it mattered in the end.
For when I set out to untangle
The deepest insecurities that bound me,
Handcuffed to the bed of low self-esteem,
I found confidence and self-respect
Whisked together like cake batter,
Feeding themselves to me,
Like life to a statue,
Like fire to ice.

immortal

If the stories of people's lives were food for
my soul,
The poems they wrote were a water bowl.
If their music comforted me like a softly
made bed,
And their kindness wrapped me up like
threads;
If my fears were erased by floral sparkles,
And our wounds were healed by our morals;
If the moon alone could make my woes
darkle,
Then I'd long to be immortal.

on days when I don't betray my mother tongue

Yé vasl-o-hijr kā silsilā hai zindagī,
Miló to tum mere,
Bichhdó to tumhārī main.
Kash-ma-kash hai aisī,
Ki ghabrāhat hai umas jaisī.
Samay bīté to lagtā hai,
Ham ēk dōsrē kē
Thahrē, to kisī kē nahīṅ.

ये वस्ल-ओ-हिज़्र का सिलसिला है ज़िंदगी,
मिलो तो तुम मेरे,
बिछड़ो तो तुम्हारी मैं।
कशमकश है ऐसी,

कि घबराहट है उमस जैसी।
समय बीते तो लगता है,
हम एक-दूसरे के,
ठहरे, तो किसी के नहीं।

how I found my God

I sit in a room with stillness,
heavy with the opposite of meaning.
Nothing moves unless I will it—
when did I become its god?

The curtain sways in quiet rebellion,
and the dreamcatcher from college still dares
to dream,
though I can't remember what for.

There's a book, spine broken,
stuck on the page I last touched.
It doesn't ache for my return,

doesn't resent being abandoned.
It waits, like everything else.
As if to remind me,
I am its god.

My backpack glares from the corner,
perhaps weary of journeys that always circle
back to this stillness.
Bundles of clothes whisper softly,
begging me to see there's no perfect moment
ahead—
only now, only this skin,
only this chance to adorn myself with care.

The vitamin bottles stand half-empty,
their promises as hollow as mine.
Utensils from last night's ramen stand idle,
wishing with me that I'd write a few words
before letting sleep take me.
Photos, trapped in their frames,
remind me that time is both mother and
thief.
The towel, damp and tired,
knows me better than I know myself.

Everything here sees me.

It's not the walls that keep my secrets,
but all the things I call mine.

Their gazes are piercing,
so sharp I nearly beg them to turn away.

In their silent servitude,
they hold me
until they see so much of me
that they become my gods.

Everything becomes my god.

And I hope they know,
I notice them,
I worship them.